Stringtastic
BOOK 1 : DOUBLE BASS

Mark Wilson and Paul Wood
With illustrations by Sarah-Leigh Wills

For online backing tracks scan the QR code
or go to fabermusic.com/audio

Contents

1. Time for C! 4
2. Deep feelings 4
3. Gee up! 5
4. Welly Bob shuffle 5
5. Boogie bow 6
6. C air 7
7. Into the deep C 7
8. Bassers and chasers 8
9. City of dust 8
10. Listen 9
11. Flowing downstream 10
12. Happy and free 10
13. Be a butterfly 11
14. When the world has gone to sleep 12
15. A hint of jasmine 12
16. Smoothly does it 13
17. Blue sky 14
18. Sometimes 15
19. Sticky toffee pudding 16
20. Clever cat 17
21. Come and play with us 18
22. Dotty's dotted notes 18
23. Playtime 19
24. Quiver of eighths 19
25. Higgledy-piggledy 20
26. Ducks on a pond 21
27. Hide-and-seek 21
28. Jig together 22
29. Dark forest 22
30. Four great friends 23
31. Bullfrog rant 23
32. Come, let's dance! 24
33. The fly's reply 24
34. Light of the moon 25
35. Thinking back 26
36. A dance for Dorian 27
37. Side by side
38. What to do? 28
39. Deep in the heart of the forest 28
40. Eggy soldiers! 29
41. Let shine your light 30
42. Flying 31
43. Echo location 31
44. Down in the dumps 31
45. Little waltz 32
46. Far and near 32
47. Are you sure it's sharp? 32
48. Back and forth 33
49. Mini minuet 33
50. Spring into action 33
51. Bowing free and easy 34
52. Dot and Spot 35
53. Showtime! 36
54. Twinkling waltz 37
55. The pirates 38
56. Early one morning 39
57. Worm dance 40

All music and lyrics by Mark Wilson and Paul Wood unless otherwise stated. With thanks to our double bass consultant, Lesley-Ann Smith.

The rights of Mark Wilson and Paul Wood to be identified as the joint authors of this work, and of Sarah-Leigh Wills to be identified as the creator of page illustrations in this work, have been asserted in accordance with the Copyright, Designs and Patents Act, 1988.

© 2022 by Faber Music Ltd
First published by Faber Music Ltd
Bloomsbury House, 74–77 Great Russell Street, London WC1B 3DA
Music processed by Donald Thomson
Cover design by WattGenius Creative
Page design by Chloë Alexander
Page illustrations by Sarah-Leigh Wills
Printed in England by Caligraving Ltd
All rights reserved
ISBN10: 0-571-54258-1
EAN13: 978-0-571-54258-1

To buy Faber Music publications or to find out about the full range of titles available please contact your local music retailer or Faber Music sales enquiries:

Faber Music Ltd, Burnt Mill, Elizabeth Way, Harlow CM20 2HX
Tel: +44 (0) 1279 82 89 82
fabermusic.com

Learn as you play through the world of *Stringtastic!*

Stringtastic Book 1 is an exciting collection of fun new compositions covering a wide range of styles. These pieces are progressively presented, taking the player on a journey from the D major scale through to Grade 1 (Early Elementary) level. No more than one technique is introduced at a time and space is given for consolidation.

These books have been designed for maximum flexibility:

- *Stringtastic Book 1* for violin, viola, cello and double bass is fully integrated to work together in any combination – ideal for use in individual lessons as well as group lessons and string orchestras.

- Many tunes have fun lyrics to sing, helping to develop a strong sense of pitch and rhythm. Learners can try writing their own lyrics, too!

- Dynamics are given throughout, but players are encouraged to add their own once a confident sound has been developed. Where there are lyrics, dynamics have consistently been placed below the lyric line and apply to both parts in the duets.

- Fingering is provided to aid the player but is all discretionary and flexible.

- While there are 57 pieces in total, eight of these are equal-level duets, both accompanied and unaccompanied; here players are encouraged to learn both parts.

- Every tune has a fun backing track to play along to, as well as a piano-only backing track for practice:

 Scan the QR code or go to fabermusic.com/audio to download the tracks.

3. Gee up!

4. Welly Bob shuffle

5. Boogie bow

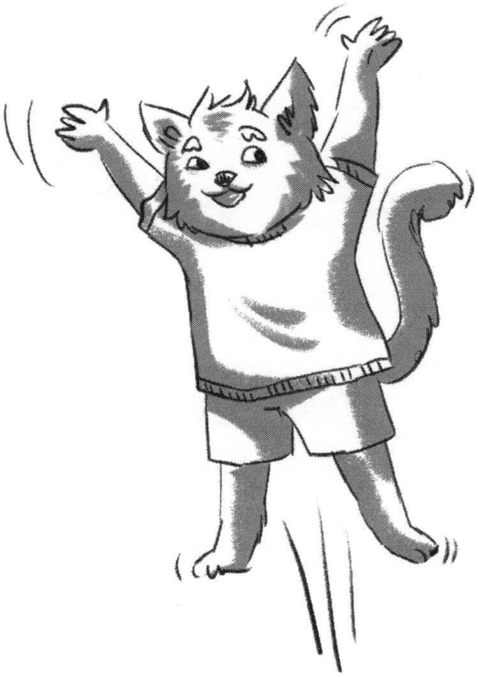

With energy ♩ = 112—138

Count 4 bars

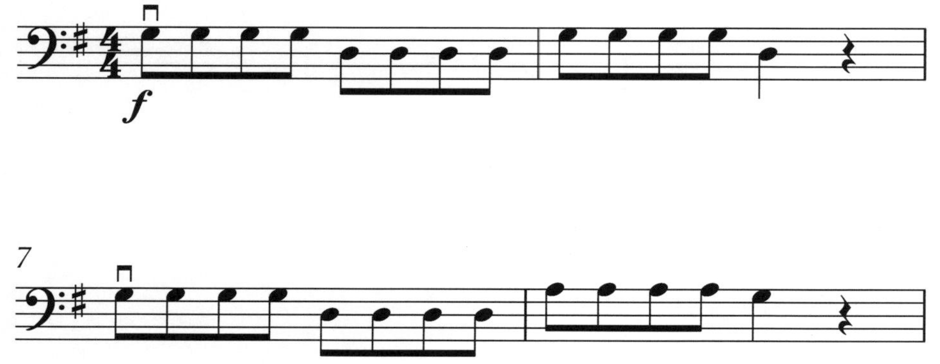

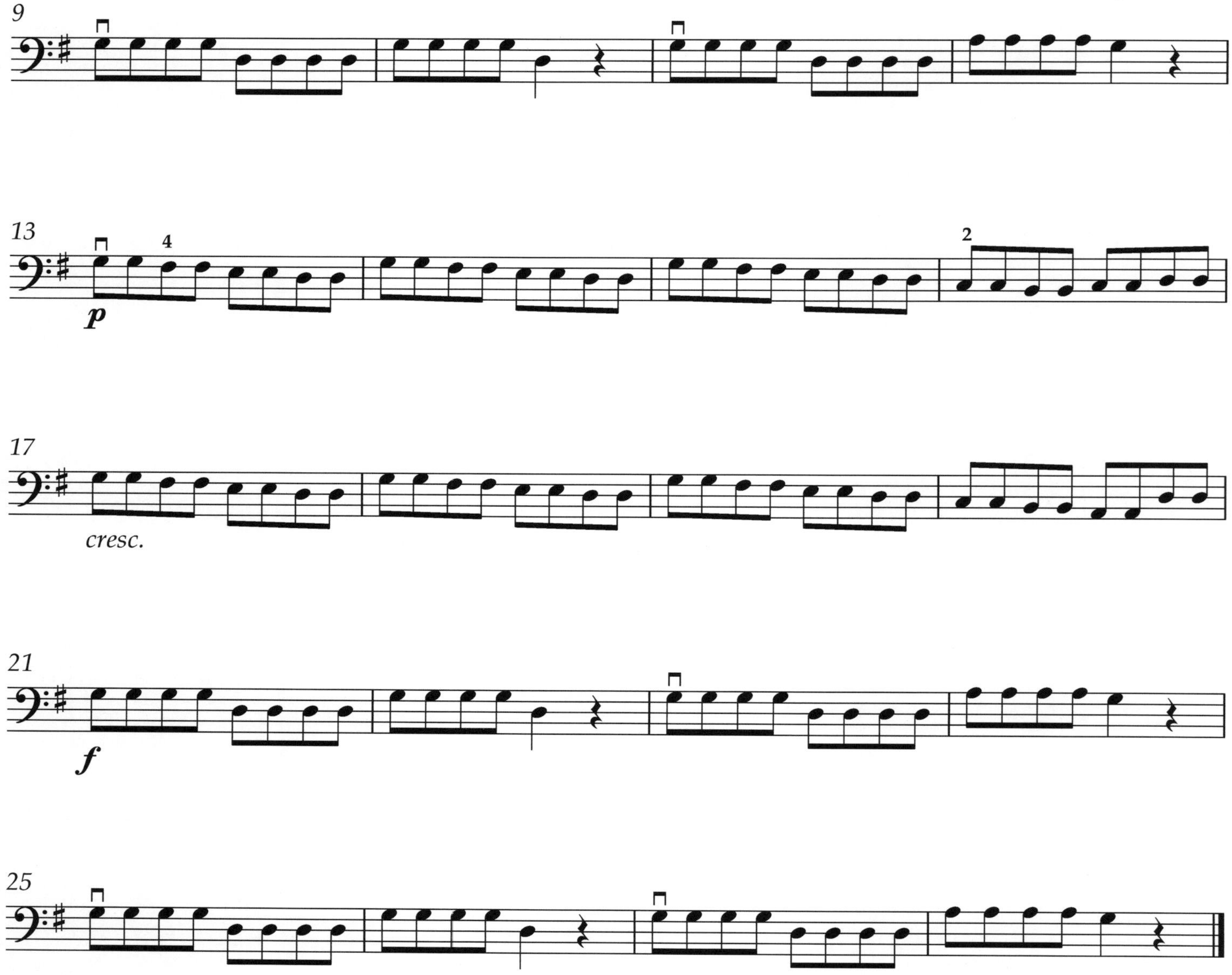

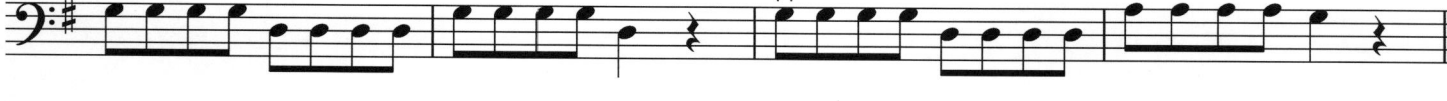

8. Bassers and chasers

We are bass-ers and we're chas-ers …

9. City of dust

10. Listen

11. Flowing downstream

Flowing ♩ = 80

Count 2 bars

12. Happy and free

Dancing ♩ = 92—120

Count 2 bars

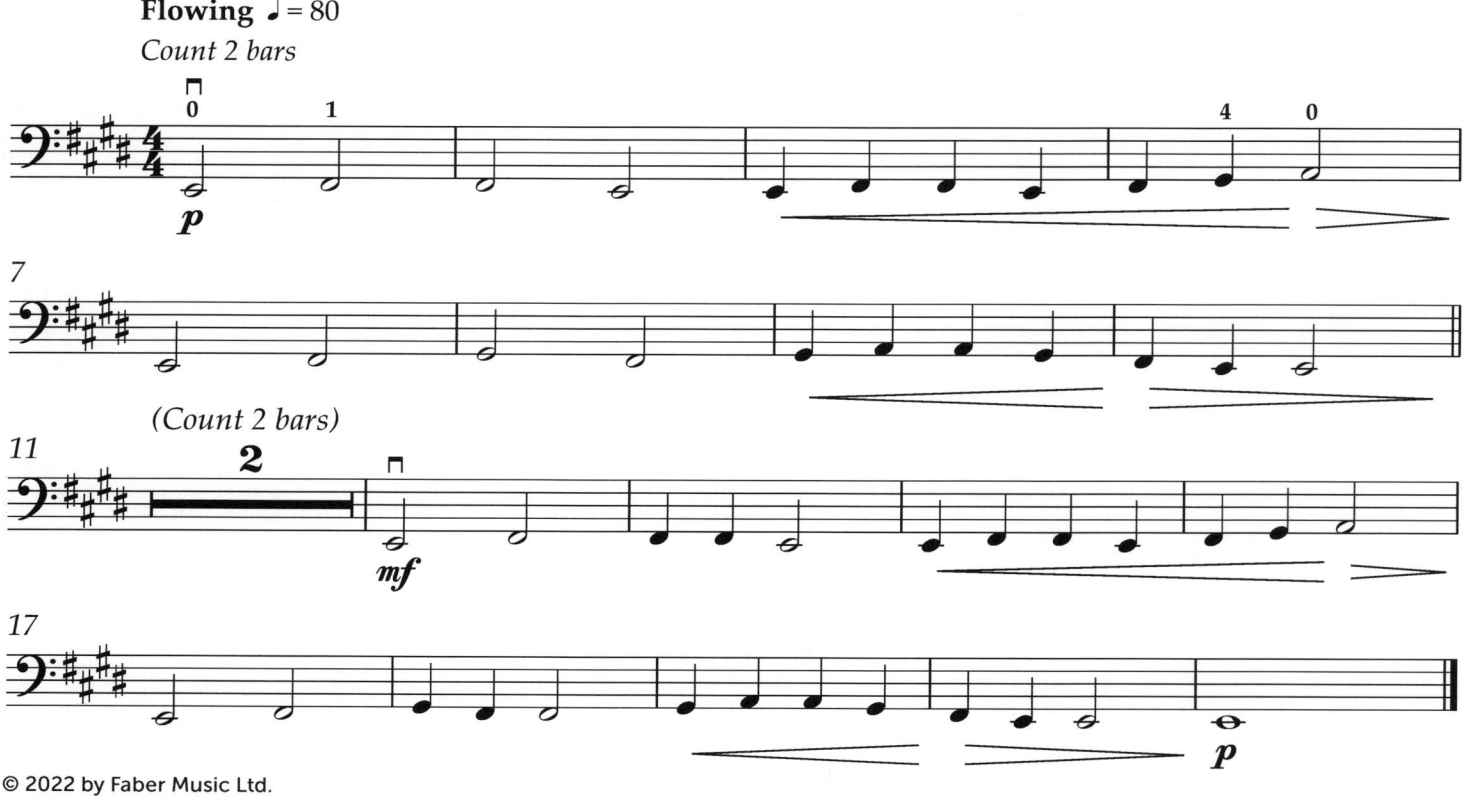

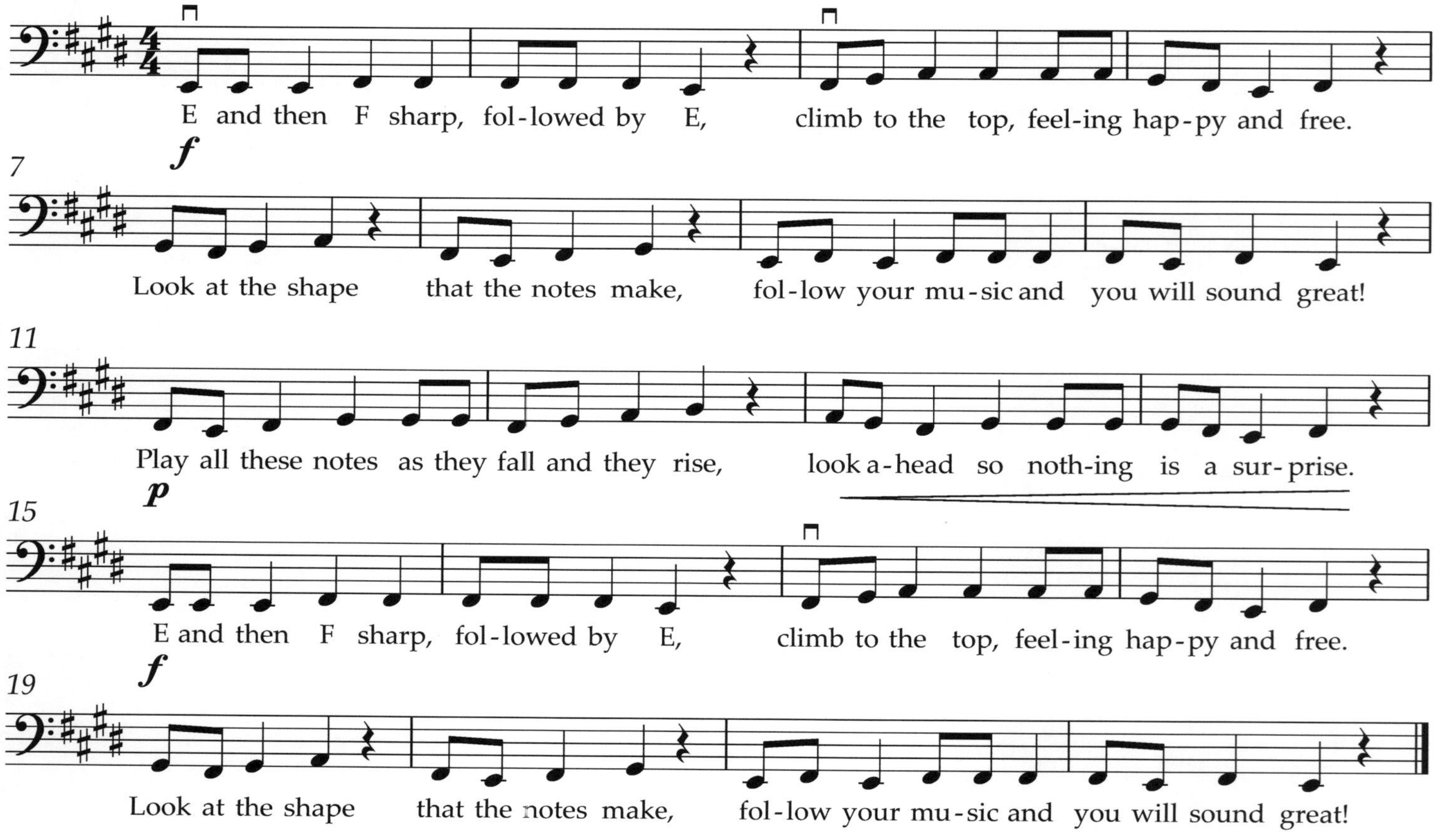

13. Be a butterfly

Flighty ♩ = 100
Count 2 bars

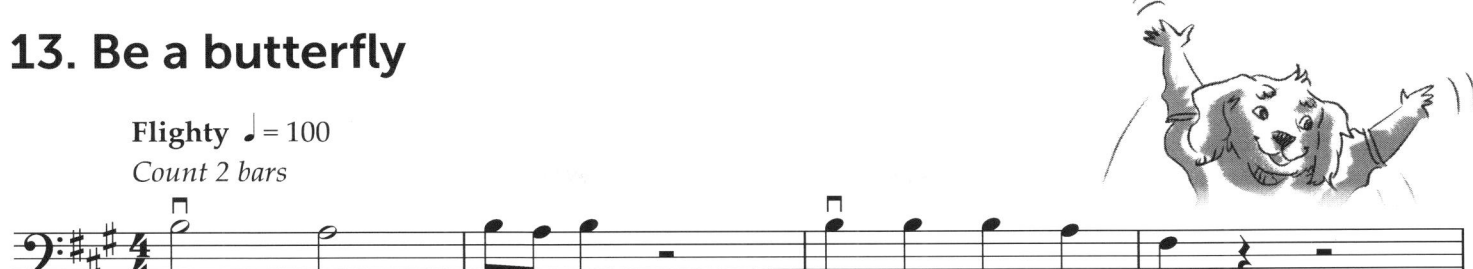
Be a but-ter-fly, rea-dy to take off.

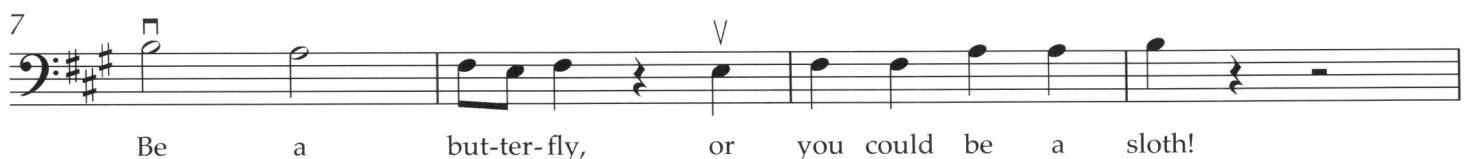
Be a but-ter-fly, or you could be a sloth!

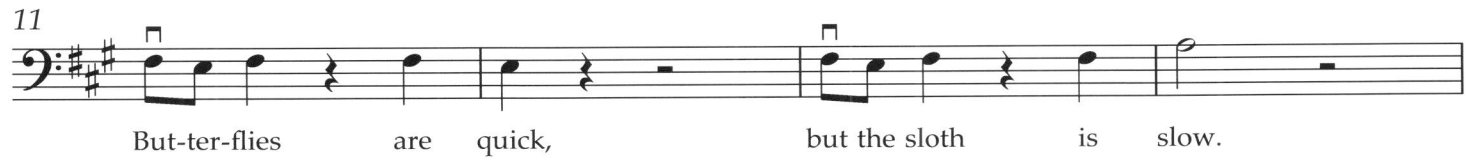
But-ter-flies are quick, but the sloth is slow.

But-ter-flies, they spread their wings and, flut-ter-ing, they go. But

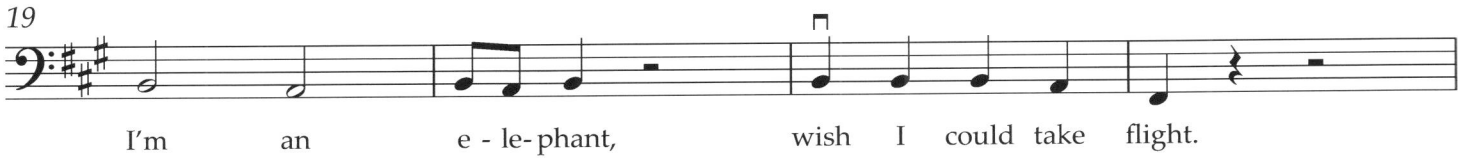
I'm an e-le-phant, wish I could take flight.

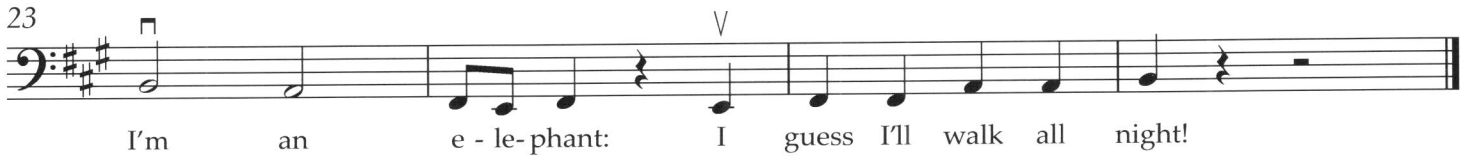
I'm an e-le-phant: I guess I'll walk all night!

© 2022 by Faber Music Ltd.

14. When the world has gone to sleep

Like a hymn ♩ = 76—92
Count 2 bars

When the world has gone to sleep, all the peo-ple count-ing sheep,
I'm a-wake in my bed, writ-ing mu-sic in my head.
Then, at last, sleep draws near and the tunes dis-ap-pear.
When I wake they've flown a-way, chased off by the break of day.
Stretch and yawn!
Mu-sic where have you gone? You have van-ished with the dawn.

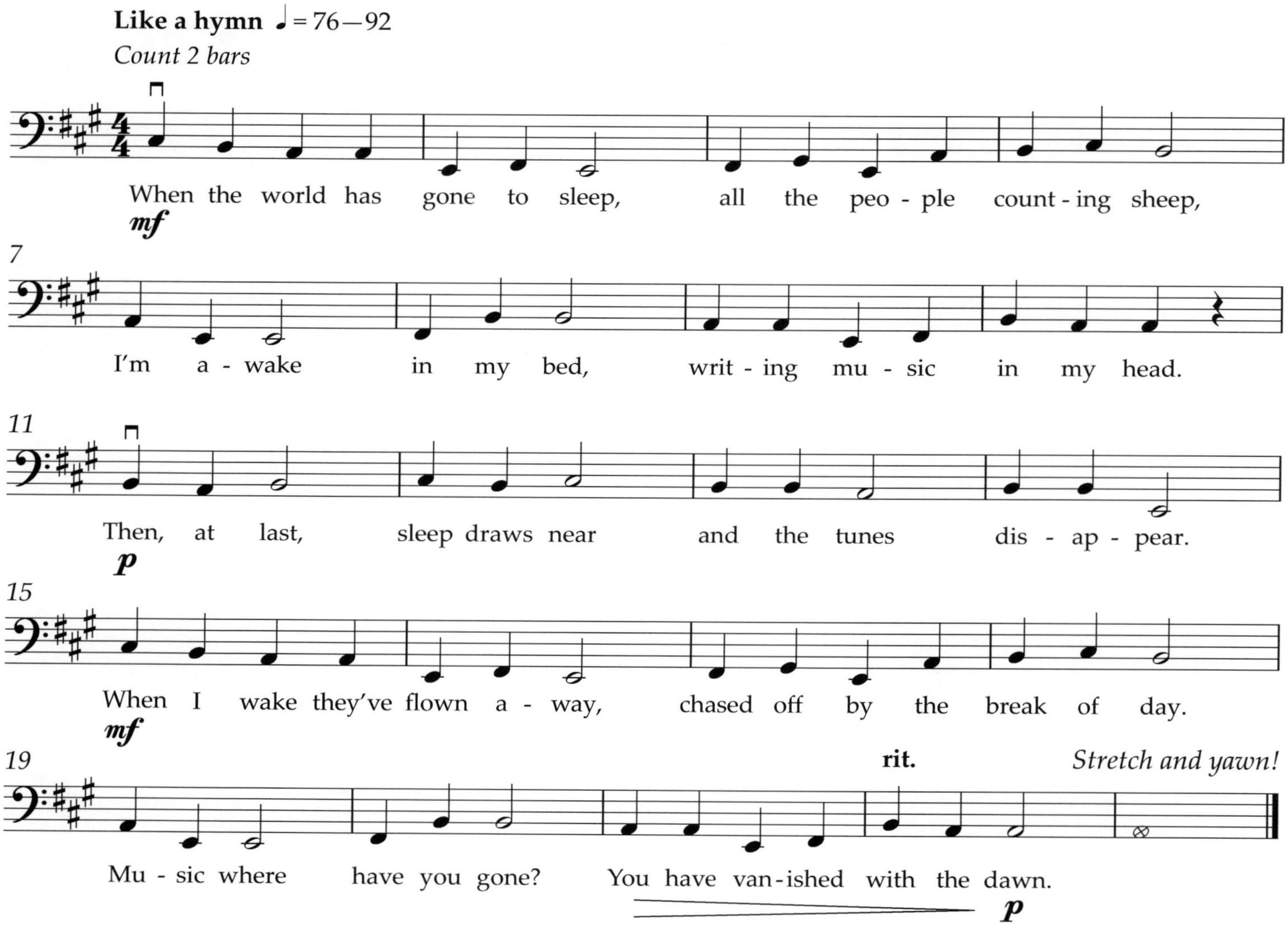

© 2022 by Faber Music Ltd.

15. A hint of jasmine

Gently swaying ♩ = 66—88
Count 2 bars

© 2022 by Faber Music Ltd.

16. Smoothly does it

18. Sometimes

19. Sticky toffee pudding

Enthusiastically ♩ = 60–76

Count 2 bars

Sti - cky tof - fee pud - ding, pep - pe - ro - ni piz - za, **f**

stacked up on my plate, that does look yum - my.

Shep - herd's pie and cus - tard, broc - co - li and choc - 'late,

topped off with some rhu - barb in my tum - my.

When my plate is clean my bel - ly starts to rum - ble, **p**

I can hear it grum - ble, I don't know why!

Run - ning from the ta - ble, head - ing for the bath - room, **f**

hop - ing I'm in time 'cause I FEEL SICK!

© 2022 by Faber Music Ltd.

20. Clever cat

With *feline!* ♩ = 66–84
Count 2 bars

21. Come and play with us

22. Dotty's dotted notes

23. Playtime

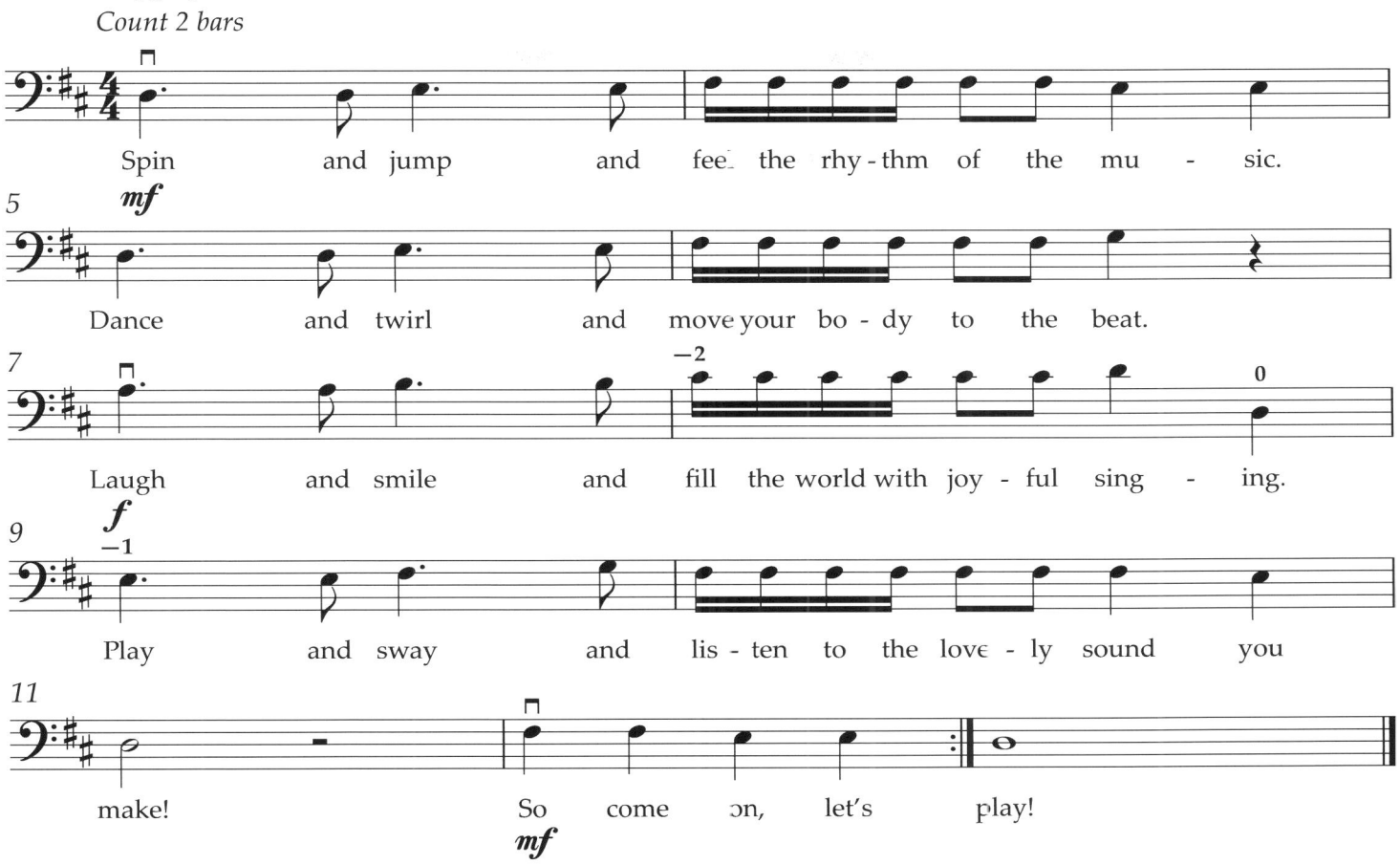

© 2022 by Faber Music Ltd.

24. Quiver of eighths

© 2022 by Faber Music Ltd.

25. Higgledy-piggledy

26. Ducks on a pond

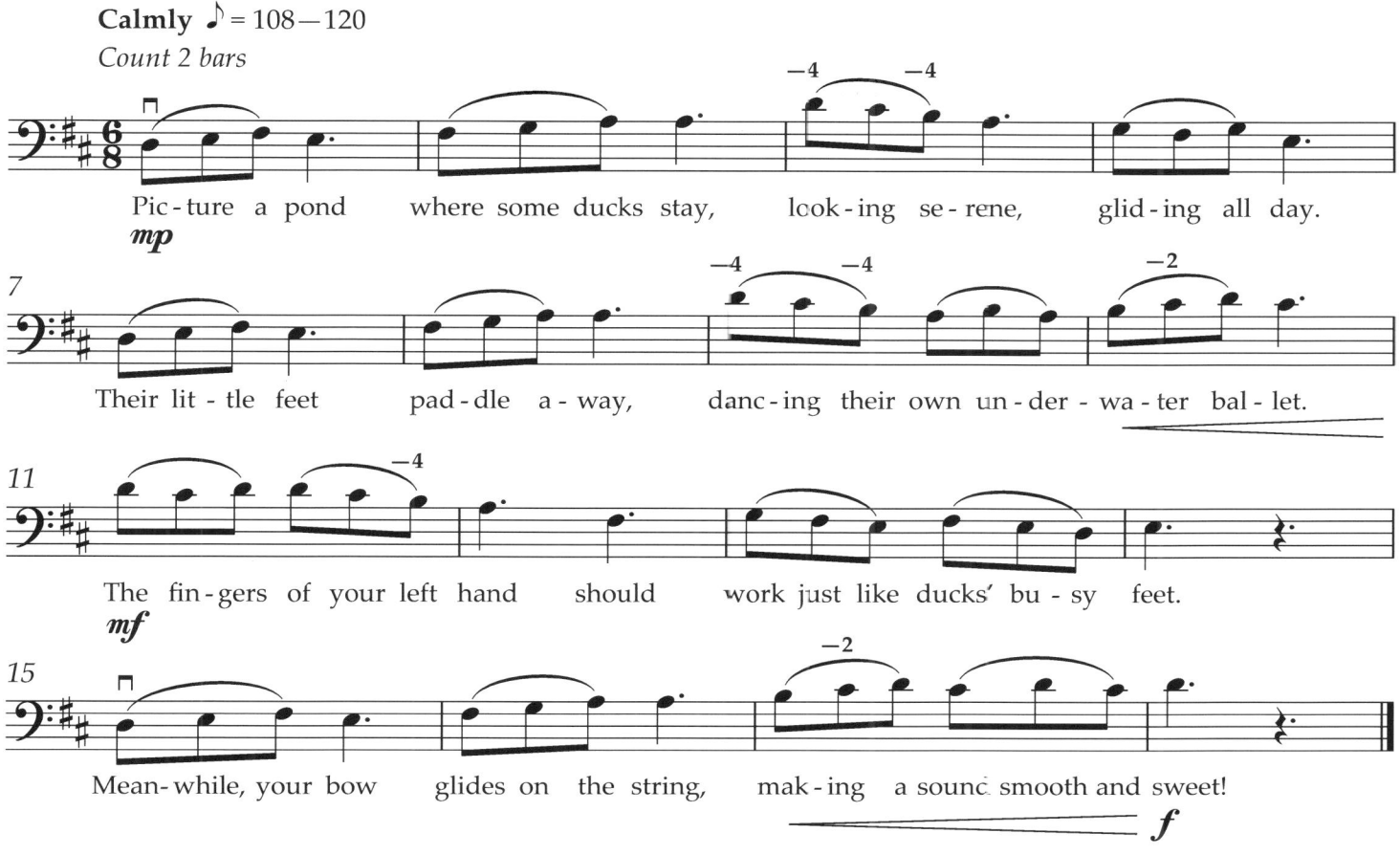

27. Hide-and-seek

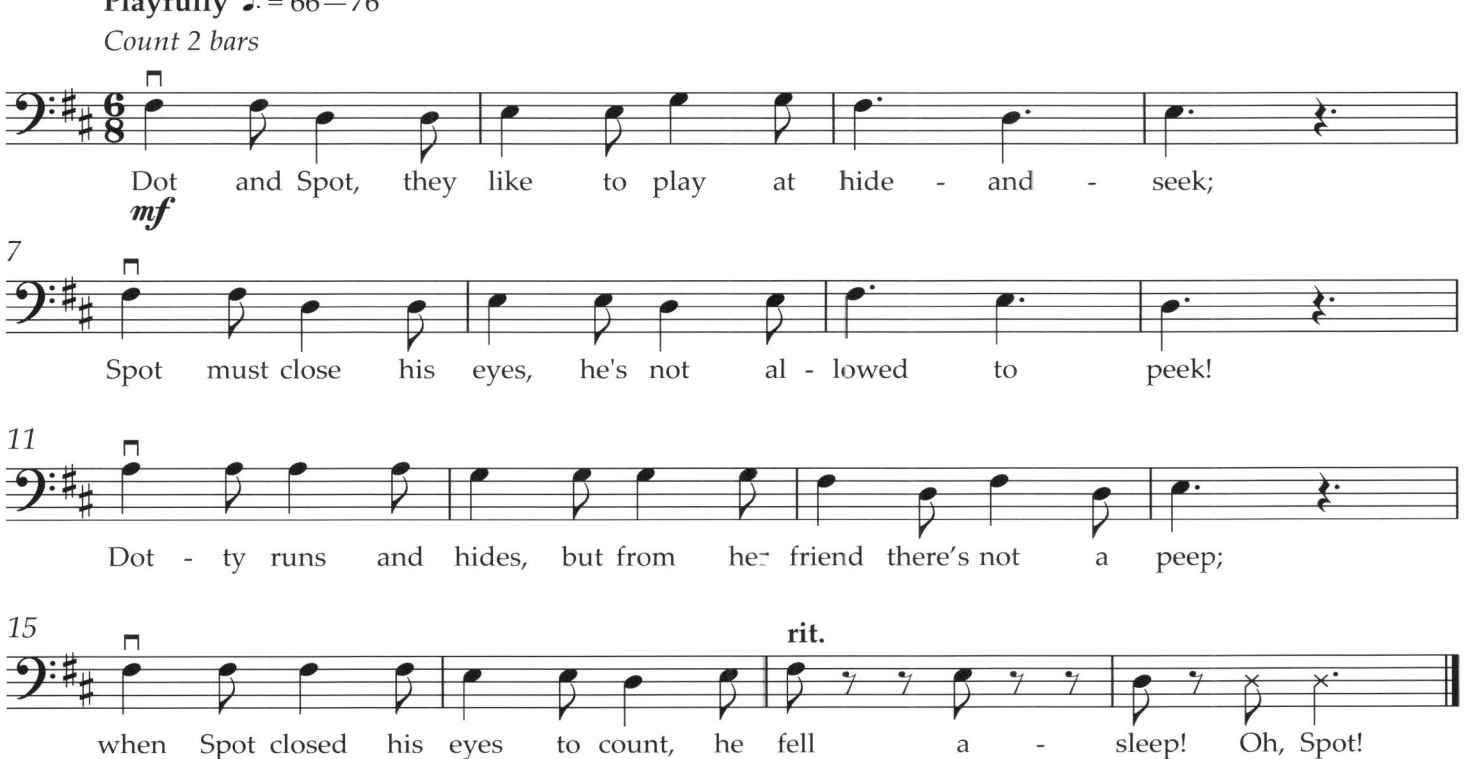

28. Jig together

With lift ♩. = 63—80

29. Dark forest

Darkly ♩ = 76
Count 2 bars

© 2022 by Faber Music Ltd.

32. Come, let's dance!

33. The fly's reply Ode to a bullfrog!

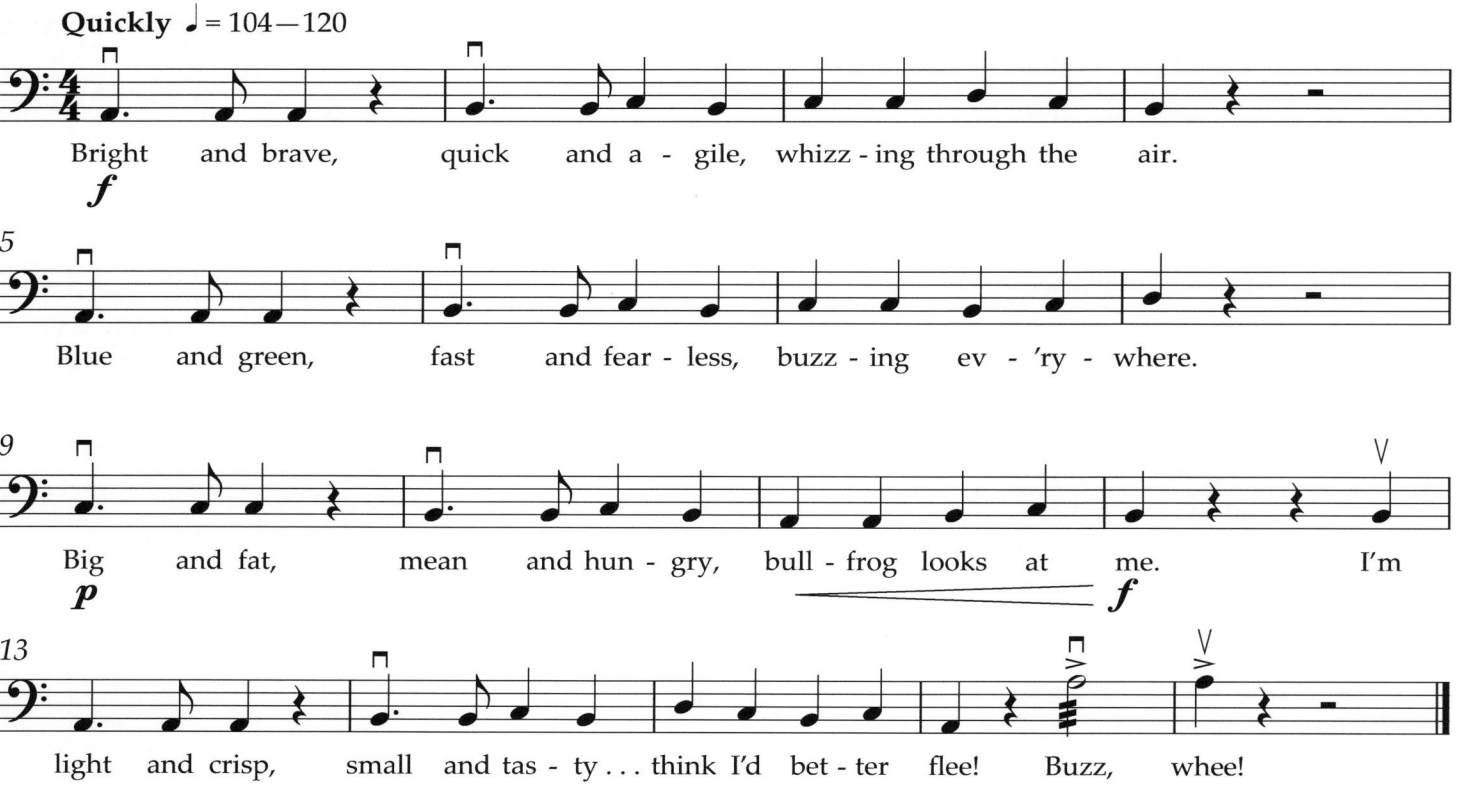

34. Light of the moon

Gently ♩ = 72
Count 2 bars

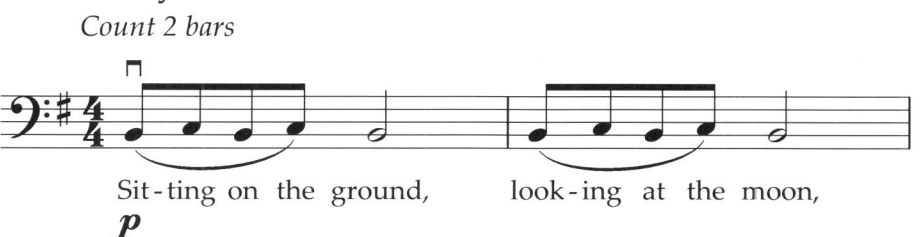

Sit-ting on the ground, look-ing at the moon,
p

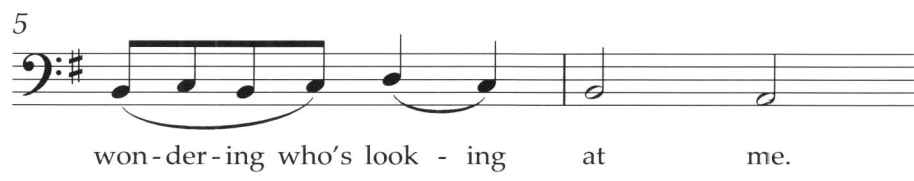

won-der-ing who's look-ing at me.

Won-der what they see, look-ing down on me, hope they see my beam-ing smile!

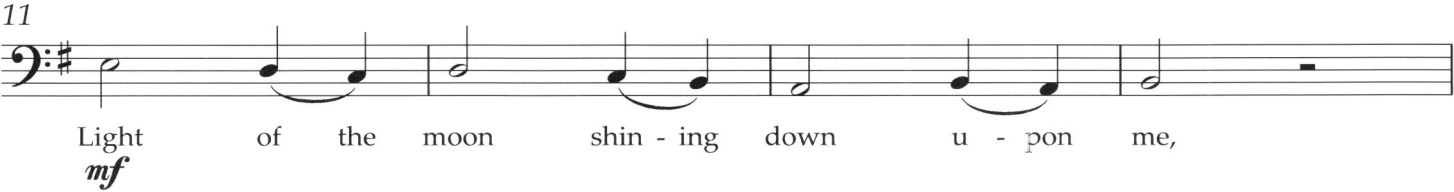

Light of the moon shin-ing down u-pon me,
mf

light up my smile so the whole world can see.

Smil-ing at the moon, wish-ing you were here, light-ing up the world with me.
p

© 2022 by Faber Music Ltd.

35. Thinking back

38. What to do?

39. Deep in the heart of the forest

40. Eggy soldiers!

Lyrics trad.

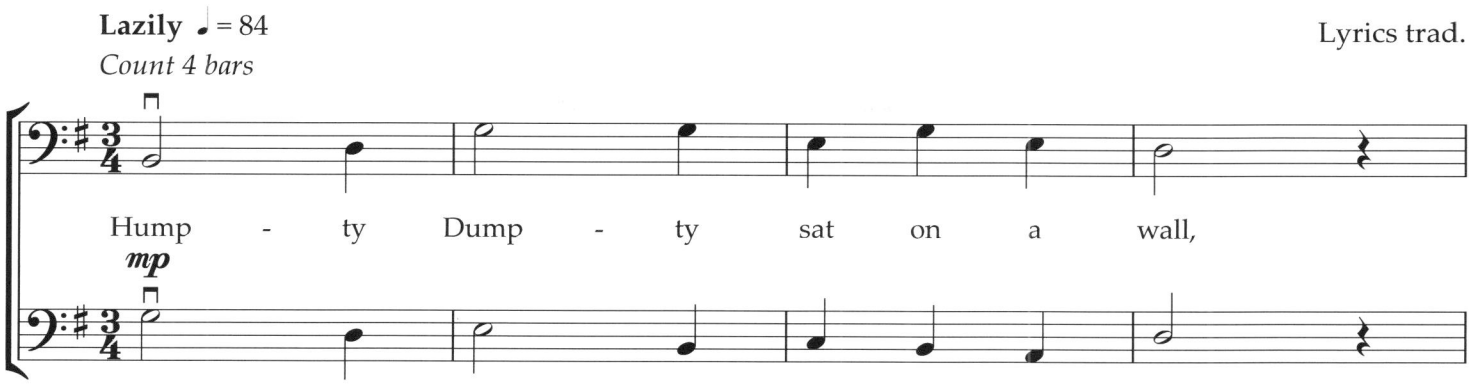

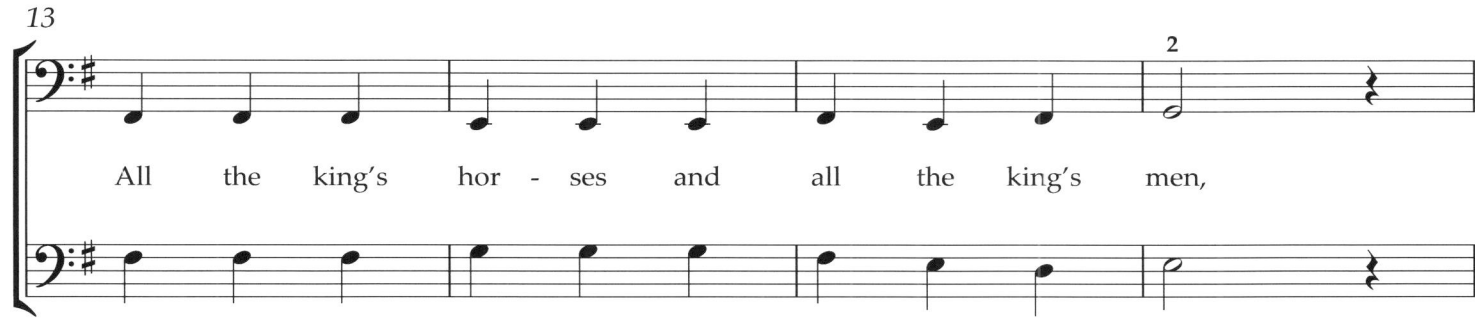
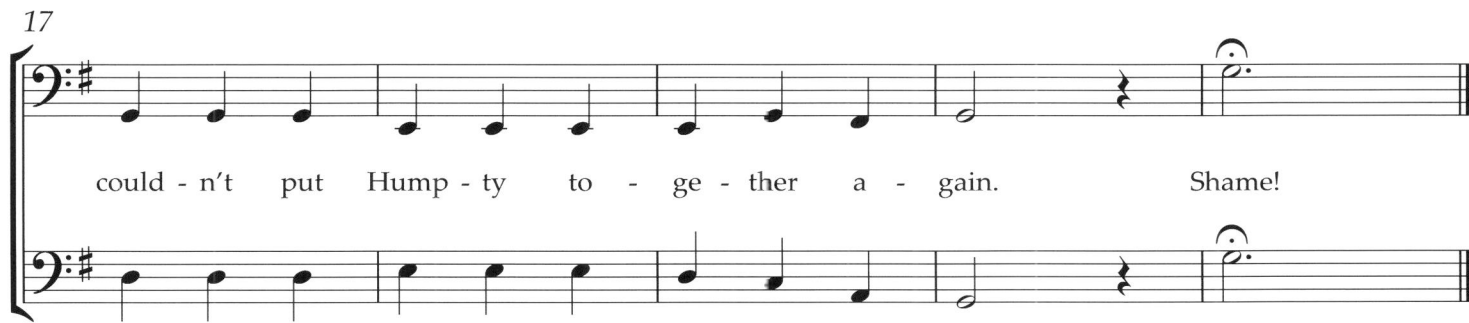

© 2022 by Faber Music Ltd.

41. Let shine your light

42. Flying

43. Echo location

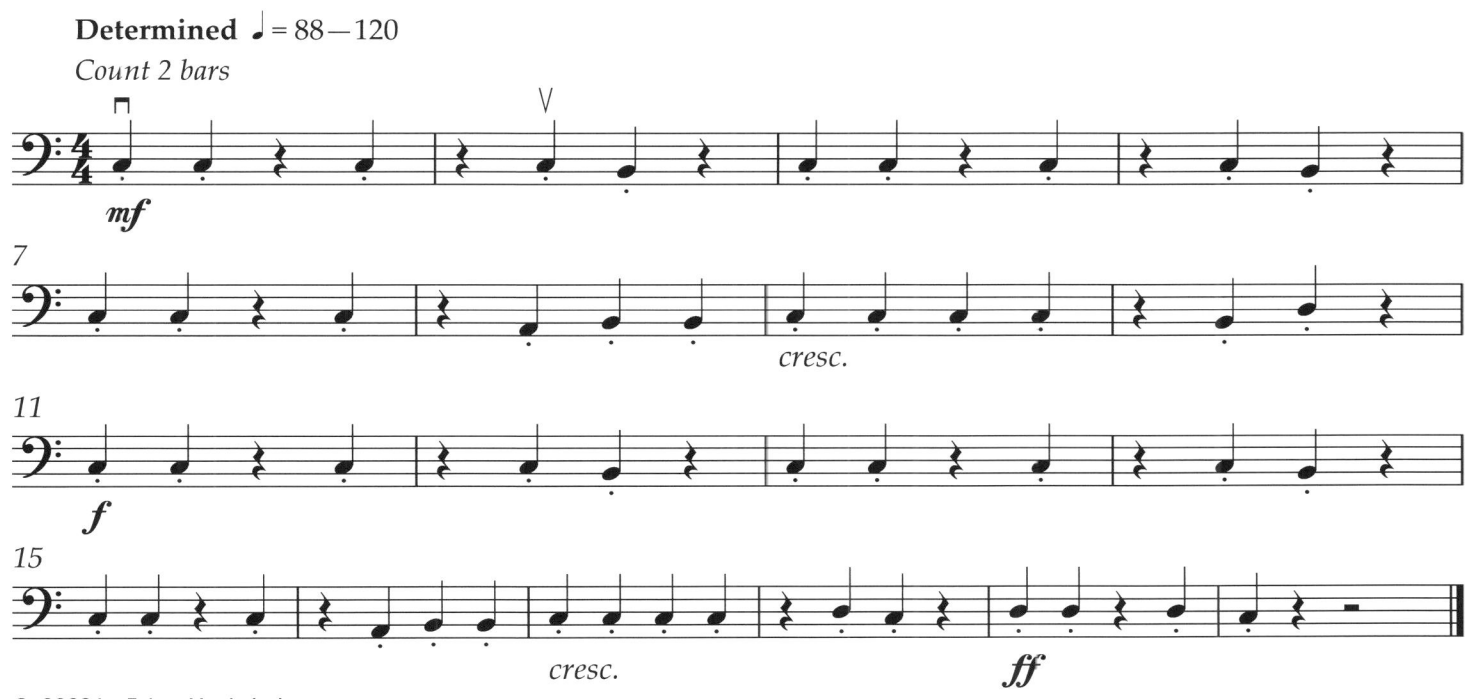

44. Down in the dumps

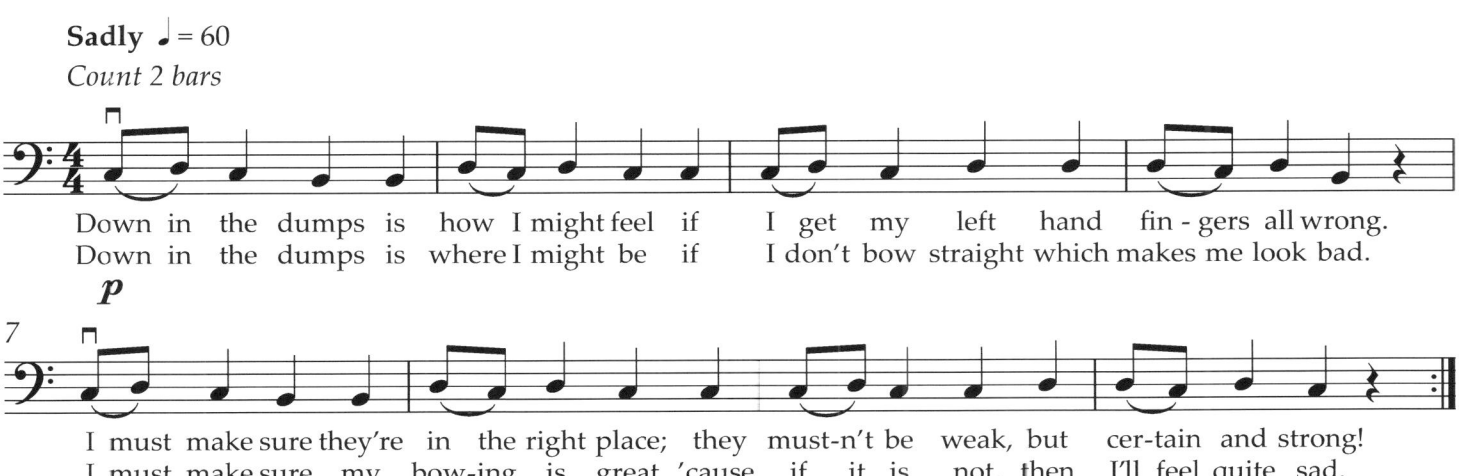

Down in the dumps is how I might feel if I get my left hand fin-gers all wrong.
Down in the dumps is where I might be if I don't bow straight which makes me look bad.

I must make sure they're in the right place; they must-n't be weak, but cer-tain and strong!
I must make sure my bow-ing is great, 'cause if it is not, then I'll feel quite sad.

45. Little waltz

Slow waltz tempo ♩ = 92—100
Count 2 bars

46. Far and near

With precision ♩ = 88
Count 2 bars

47. Are you sure it's sharp?

Gently ♩ = 48

Is it sharp? Yes it is! Is it sharp? No it's not!
Are you sure that it's sharp? Is it sharp? It is not!
When it's sharp 4 comes to play, when it's not, then 2's the way!
In this piece the sharps sound bright; na-tu-rals turn off the light. Is it sharp?

48. Back and forth

With feeling ♩ = 63—72
Count 2 bars

All Fs are sharp in this song, Cs are not, so don't go wrong!
D string's where F sharps all stay, A string has no sharps to play.

© 2022 by Faber Music Ltd.

49. Mini minuet

Dancing ♩ = 112—120
Count 4 bars

© 2022 by Faber Music Ltd.

50. Spring into action

Lively ♩ = 84—92

© 2022 by Faber Music Ltd.

51. Bowing free and easy

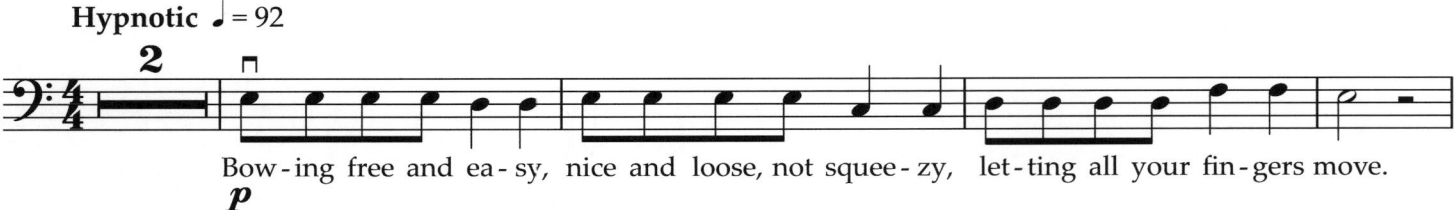
Bow-ing free and ea-sy, nice and loose, not squee-zy, let-ting all your fin-gers move.

Don't hold your bow tight-ly, just play ve-ry light-ly, then you'll make a sound so smooth.

Try to play quite near the fin-ger-board to hear the qui-et sound that suits this song.

Keep the mu-sic flow-ing with pre-ci-sion bow-ing, whe-ther notes are short or long.

Though the sound is grow-ing, just re-lax your bow-ing, that will let the mu-sic sing.

Short notes need a small bow, long notes: let your arm go, then you'll get your sound to ring.

Some-thing else to men-tion: play-ing with-out ten-sion makes a per-fect bow-ing arm.

Bow-ing free and ea-sy, nice and loose, not squee-zy, that will work just like a charm!

© 2022 by Faber Music Ltd.

52. Dot and Spot

53. Showtime!

54. Twinkling waltz

55. The pirates

56. Early one morning

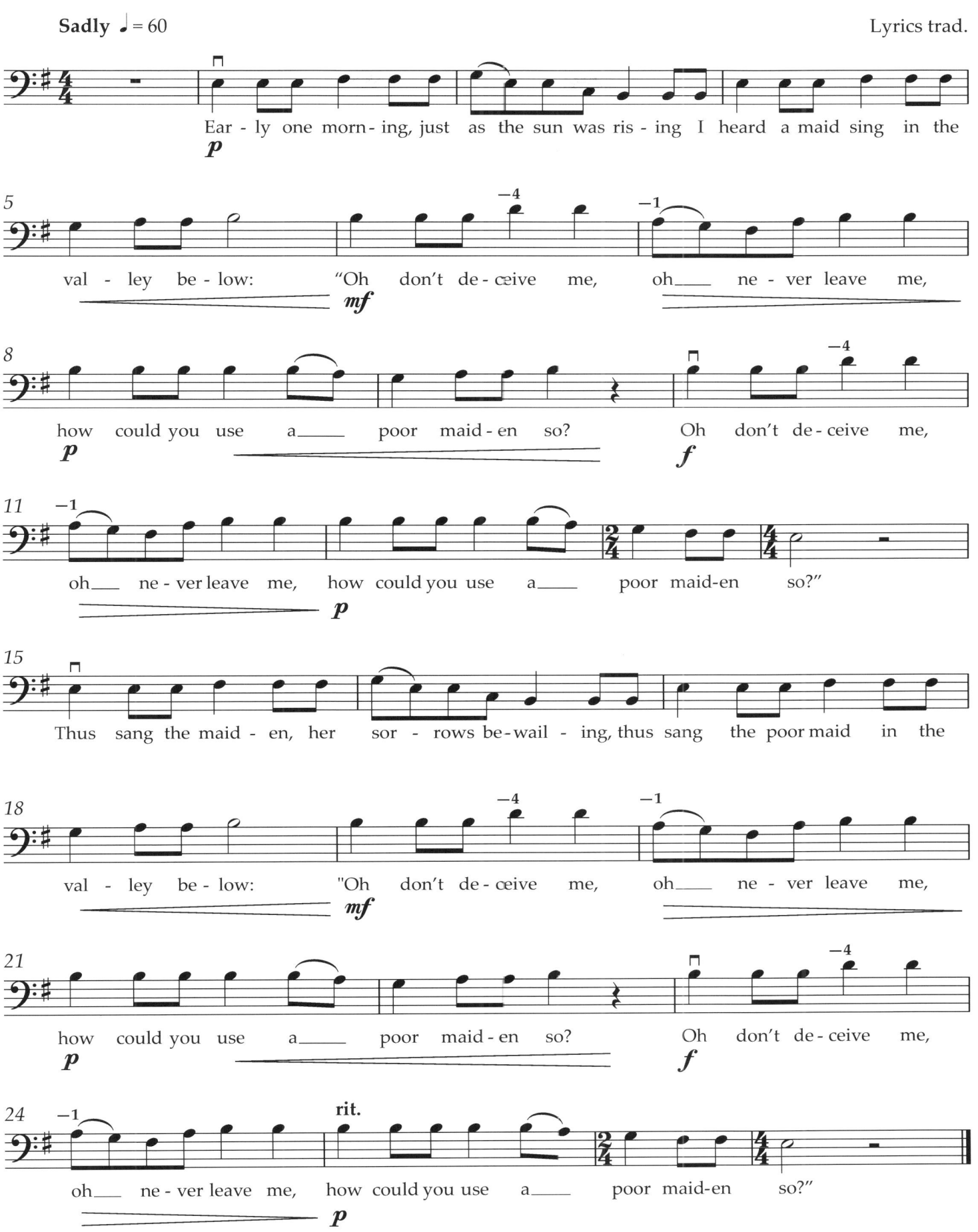

57. Worm dance